Bearing Up

ISBN 0 947338 78 0

Copyright © Axiom Publishing
First Edition 1996
Reprinted 1996 (twice), 1997

This edition reprinted 1997 exclusivety for Selecta Book Ltd.
Folly Road, Roundway, Devises, Wiltshire, UK.

Bearing Up

Illustrations:-
Mike Johnson

*If we might have a second
chance
To live the days once more,
And rectify mistakes we've made
To even up the score.*

*If we might have a second
chance
To use the knowledge gained,
Perhaps we might become at last
As fine as God ordained.*

*But though we can't retrace our
steps,
However stands the score,
Tomorrow brings another
chance,
For us to try once more.*

If all good people were clever,
And all clever people were good,
The world would be nicer than ever
We thought that it possibly could.

But somehow, 'tis seldom or never
The two hit it off as they should;
The good are so harsh to the clever,
The clever so rude to the good.

Elizabeth Wordsworth

*We should not
let the grass grow
on the path of
friendship.*

Marie Therese Rodet Geoffrin

*We share our happiness with
each other -
and it becomes greater.
We share our troubles with
each other -
and they become smaller.
We share one another's griefs
and burdens -
and their weight becomes
possible to bear.*

For if a man should dream
of heaven and,
waking, find
within his hand a flower
as token that he
had really been there -
what then,
what then?

Thomas Wolfe

Oh, to be only half as wonderful
as my child thought I was
when he was small,
and only half as stupid
as my teenager now thinks I am.

Rebecca Richards

Happiness
is not a state to arrive at,
but a manner of travelling.

Margaret Lee Runbeck

*To a heart formed for
friendship and affection
the charms of solitude
are very short-lived.*

Fanny Burney

'Tis easy enough to be pleasant,
When life flows by like a song;
But the man worthwhile,
Is the man with a smile,
When everything goes dead
wrong.

Ella Wheeler Wilcox

This above all -
to thine own self be true,
And it must follow,
as the night the day,
Thou canst not then
be false to any man.

William Shakespeare

Help me to be
Cheerful
when things go wrong;
Persevering
when things are difficult;
and serene
when things are irritating.

Two men trod the way of life;
The first, with downcast eye;
The second with an eager face
Uplifted to the sky.

He who gazed upon the ground
said, 'Life is dull and gray,'
But he who looked into the stars
Went singing on his way.

*To know that others
have walked
a similar road may
not make the difficulties
of the journey easier,
but should give us hope.*

No one ever
ruined their eyesight -
by looking on
the bright side.

Who walks in a rut walks alone
Ruts grow deeper and deeper:
There's only room for one in a rut,
Walls rise steeper and steeper.
Soon he's lonely lost to view,
Soon he can't see over
To where his friends of yesterday
Are walking in fields of clover.

I'm not going to worry
Unless the animals
start lining up
two by two
for the next
space shuttle!

*The only reward of
virtue is virtue;
the only way to have
a friend is to
be one.*

Ralph Waldo Emerson

Remember,
no one can make
you feel inferior
without your consent.

Eleanor Roosevelt

*If you see someone
without a smile
give them one.*

*A pessimist
is one who blows out
the light
to see how dark it is.*

*Do you know
how helpless you feel
if you have a
full cup of coffee
in your hand and
you start to sneeze.*

Jean Kerr

*Those who say it
can't be done
shouldn't stand
in the way of
those who are
doing it.*

You can make more friends
in two months by becoming
interested in other people,

*than you can in two years
by trying to get other people
interested in you.*

Dale Carnegie

When you come
to the end of your rope.
Tie a knot in it
and hold on.

The balm of life,
a kind and faithful friend.

Mercy Otis Warren

Never look for the faults
as you go through life,
and even when you find them,
it is right and kind
to be somewhat blind,
and look for the virtues
behind them.

Love your enemy -
it will drive him nuts.

Eleanor Doan